LIONS

MARYSA STORM

BLACK
RABBIT
BOOKS

Bolt Jr. is published by Black Rabbit Books
P.O. Box 3263, Mankato, Minnesota, 56002.
www.blackrabbitbooks.com
Copyright © 2020 Black Rabbit Books

Catherine Cates, designer; Omay Ayres, photo researcher

Names: Storm, Marysa, author.
Title: Lions / by Marysa Storm.
Description: Mankato, Minnesota : Black Rabbit Books,
[2020] | Series: Bolt Jr. Awesome animal lives |
Audience: Age 6-8. | Audience: K to Grade 3. | Includes
bibliographical references and index.
Identifiers: LCCN 2018053334 (print) | LCCN 2018055076
(ebook) | ISBN 9781623101565 (e-book) |
ISBN 9781623101503 (library binding) |
ISBN 9781644661000 (paperback)
Subjects: LCSH: Lion–Juvenile literature.
Classification: LCC QL737.C23 (ebook) | LCC QL737.C23
S7926 2020 (print) | DDC 599.757–dc23
LC record available at https://lccn.loc.gov/2018053334

Printed in the United States. 5/19

Image Credits

Getty: Barcroft Media, 5; iStock: awc007, Cover; guenterguni,
16–17; National Geographic: Michael Nichols, 20–21;
Shutterstock: berry2046, 3, 24; Breaking The Walls, 22–23;
davemhuntphotography, 1; Dirk.D.Theron, 11; Eric Isselee, 4, 7,
8–9, 10, 14, 20–21; halimqd, 15; Lookingforcats, 12–13; Maggy
Meyer, 21–22; Michaell Nollta, 19–20; Raki83, 6–7; Ronel
Swanepoel, 10–11

Contents

CHAPTER 1

A Day in the Life

Three lions race through tall grass. They're chasing a zebra. Soon, the lions catch it. They claw. They bite. Their **prey** can't get away. It's lion dinnertime!

prey: an animal hunted and killed for food

WEIGHT COMPARISON

lion ◀ · · · · · · ·

265 to 560 pounds
(120 to 254 kilograms)

Big Cats

Lions are big cats. They're also powerful hunters. Lions follow prey before attacking. They use their long teeth and claws to catch it.

leopard
66 to 200 pounds
(30 to 91 kg)

PARTS OF A
Lion

fur

tail

paws

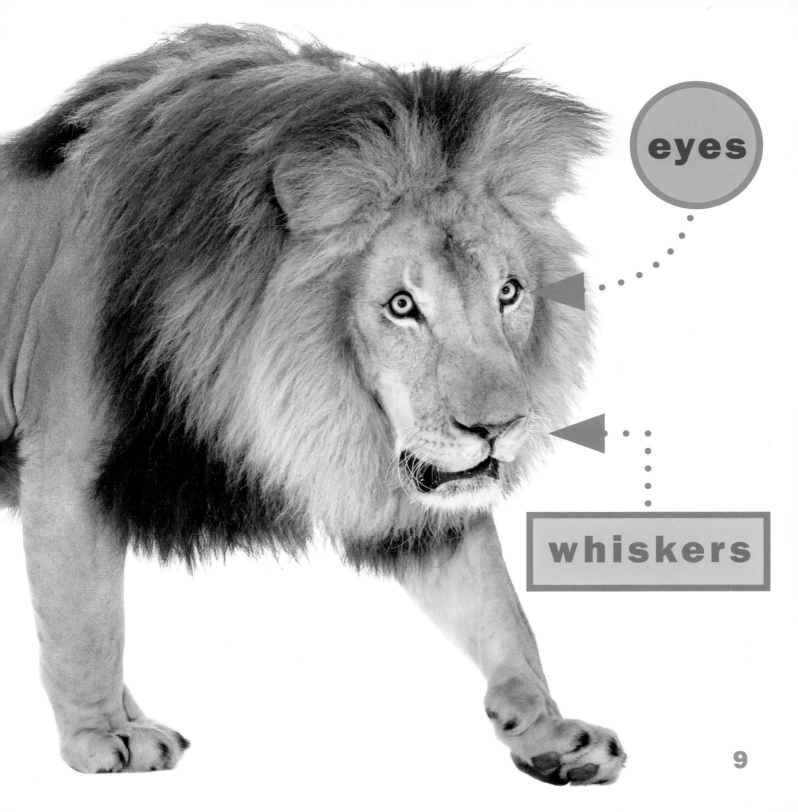

eyes

whiskers

CHAPTER 2

Food and Homes

Lions eat meat. They hunt zebras. Lions also go after birds. They eat **reptiles** too. Lions often hunt when it's mostly dark.

reptile: a cold-blooded animal that breathes air and has a backbone

FACT
Females do most of the hunting.

Lion Homes

Most lions live in Africa. Some live in open **woodlands**. Others live in **plains**. Lions stay where they can find food.

woodland: land with trees
plain: an area of land without many trees

Where Lions Live

KEY

■ = where lions live

CHAPTER 3

Family Life

Lions live in groups called prides.

Females take care of the pride's cubs.

Males protect the pride's space.

FACT

Prides usually have about 15 lions.

Babies

Female lions have cubs about every two years. They have up to six cubs.

Young cubs stay near their mothers. But they soon grow stronger. By age two, they can hunt. Then, males leave. They look for new groups. Females stay with their prides.

3

Newborn Lion's Weight
about 3 pounds
(1 kg)

Bonus Facts

Adults have 30 teeth.

Lions live **10 to 14** years.

Lions rest about 21 hours a day.

Roars can be heard 5 miles (8 kilometers) away.

roar: the loud sound of a wild animal

READ MORE/WEBSITES

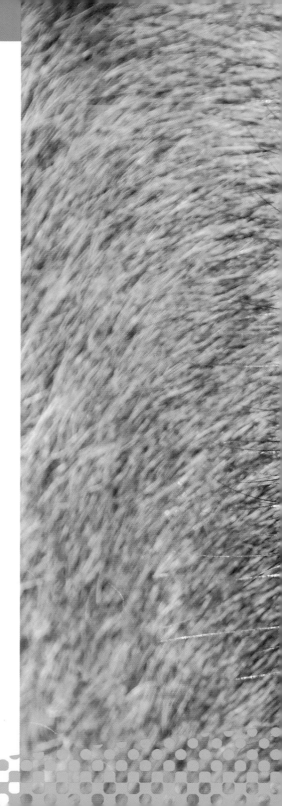

Klukow, Mary Ellen. *Lions.* African Animals. Mankato, MN: Amicus, 2020.

Riggs, Kate. *Baby Lions.* Starting Out. Mankato, MN: Creative Education, 2019.

Roome, Dr. Hugh. *Lions.* Nature's Children. New York: Children's Press, an imprint of Scholastic Inc., 2019.

African Lion
kids.sandiegozoo.org/animals/african-lion

Fun Lion Facts for Kids
www.sciencekids.co.nz/sciencefacts/animals/lion.html

Lion
kids.nationalgeographic.com/animals/lion/#ww-wild-cats-lion.jpg

GLOSSARY

plain (PLAYN)—an area of land without many trees

prey (PRAY)—an animal hunted and killed for food

reptile (REP-tile)—a cold-blooded animal that breathes air and has a backbone

roar (ROHR)—the loud sound of a wild animal

woodland (WOOD-land)—land with trees

INDEX